When the Meaning is Lost

When the Meaning is Lost

The journey through the grief, the void and the choice to live fully once again after a loss.

Jill Ethier

May this inspire you to live

♡ JE

ISBN-10: 1976188520
ISBN-13: 9781976188527

To each of you who have experienced or are experiencing any type of loss right now...

this is for you.

I have a gift for you to accompany this book, please visit www.jillethier.com/gift to receive it.

CONTENTS

Introduction: The Catalyst   3

1   When LOSS happens   14

2   First stop: The VOID   32

3   When the MEANING disappears   36

4   The IMPLOSION   40

5   Will you LIVE?   44

6   A perspective SHIFT   49

7   Your TITLE changes   55

8   The lack of understanding is HARD   58

9   The BEFORE and the AFTER   63

10   The WAY   67

11   Letting go of the WHY   73

12   KNOW this   78

13   The GIFT   82

14   Another VISIT to the void   88

15   Being forced to CHANGE   97

16   It ALL changes   104

17   It all FEELS foreign   107

18   What will you CHOOSE?   113

19   You must TRUST   121

20   Existing turns into LIVING   123

21   Continuing FORWARD   126

22   Just MOVE   129

23   Creating meaning AGAIN   134

24   Living YOUR LIFE   137

     One final thing...   145

     About the Author

Introduction:
The Catalyst

I began writing about the experiences in my life a long time ago (over eleven years ago to be more exact). Very slowly the stories and the lessons about different parts of my life have accumulated in bits and pieces over the years.

This past spring, an event happened in our lives that triggered me to dive into the writing again, to compile all of the mini-documents that I had created and to stick to my personal commitment to publish this thing. (If you are reading this, I did it...finally.)

All of what is written here has been in my mind and on my heart (as one of my best friends would say) since my baby died in 2006.

This next part in italics began as a Facebook post which I then shared in an email with my clients and friends. It was written in mid-April of 2017 and is really the catalyst for this compilation of my writing about loss (many different types of loss) since my daughter died in 2006. It is the experience that compelled me to finish writing this book.

. . . .

Subject Line of the email: What happens when your whole world changes?

Life was moving along pretty smoothly here at the acreage with things all going according to "plan". The girls were rolling along with school, activities and grad preparation (that whole thing requires a lot of outfit changes I am finding out), my business and life strategy was structured and growing and there was still lots of time and energy for extra fun events and anything that popped up. We had a plan and we were implementing it.

And then...life happened.

And it has changed everything. Nothing is the same.

Why?

Because, we aren't the same now.
It has changed what is most relevant in our world.
This event shifted the trajectory of our lives.

It made me think differently and called on EVERY skill I had to walk us through it.

And the ripple effect of the change continues to impact us as we are refocusing and moving forward based on the life that we truly want now. And based on who we are now.

Here's what happened just two weeks ago that has shifted the trajectory of our lives:

My oldest daughter (who is turning 18 in a month) was studying in her room when I received a phone call from one of my closest friends. I knew by the tone of her voice that it wasn't good.

The phone call revealed that there had been a tragic accident and my daughter's best friend had been in that accident. In a subsequent text, not even 15 short minutes later, it was confirmed that he had passed away.

My daughter's response was everything you can imagine it to be.

It was like watching someone break right before your eyes (in fact, it WAS watching someone's spirit break). As a parent, it was devastating to see that happening right in front of me. She was literally broken. She crumbled to the floor over and over again through her sobbing and streams of tears.

There was nothing to say and there was no way to stop the pain.

Her normal was no longer normal (and still isn't).

Her plans for the next few months, her grad date, her best friend and her trusted confidante were gone.

She was forced to grow up in an instant and deal with a depth of loss that some will not ever experience. As I watched her over the next few days and all of his friends at the funeral, my heart broke for all of them.

Why?

Because they were experiencing something that will forever change them.

I do believe that change and personal expansion is what life is about but this change is unexplainable, of significant impact and hard to accept and really hard to understand.

And now everything in their lives that they knew to be true....isn't anymore.

Why am I sharing this?

I created this business and working online so that I could be a very active parent when my kids needed me most. And that is, of course, what happened over these last two weeks and I am so grateful to have created this life and ability to take care of my girls when they need me most.

Most importantly, I am sharing this because I believe that transparency and sharing the hard stuff is key to growth and expansion.

I'm real. Crappy things happen. Big stuff happens and I want to share how I "handle" it and move through it. My work, my training, my personal power, my faith, my belief in the universe and my mindset has carried me through this past two weeks.

I do believe that everything does happen for a reason.

BUT...

I also believe that not every reason is clear right away and that is the hardest part of any experience like this.

*I thought that when my baby died 11 years ago, the message for me was to **live more fully** and to encourage others to do the same. I have built my business on this belief and I have created all of the programs for my clients because of it.*

I promised my baby on the day she died that I would embrace my life and honor her short life by living fully. And I feel that I have done that to the best of my ability.

*This past week though, I realized that my baby's death actually **prepared me most** for walking my oldest daughter through the death of her best friend.*

I would not have understood the grief had I not lived it.

I would not have had the depth of understanding of the pain and the void that is created had I not experienced it first hand.

And, I would not have known how nothing would feel relevant anymore after something like this unless I had walked that path.

I would not have truly understood had my second born not have died.

I can support my oldest daughter more because of my experience. These life experiences do serve us and the reason will always be revealed. Sometimes though, it takes almost 11 years to know why it happened.

Kelly, one of my clients, had this response to a question that I posted on my Facebook feed asking for your best life advice when you are going through a loss and it couldn't be truer when any BIG circumstance happens in your life...

*"...the depth of your tears, your sorrow, your fierceness of your anger now will **carve a place inside you for understanding**.*

> *You may at some point be called on by life to serve from your past pain—with a kind word, a wise nod and 'I understand what you're going through' - your word or deed may travel far with another and serve to lift them up…"*

Significant life experiences forever change us. They are meant to. We will use them to shine our light when we are called to.

I have not been the same since my baby died. It carved into me an understanding that I didn't even know I needed until 2 weeks ago.

*My oldest daughter is now going through the same life altering experience and at some point she will be called upon for her wisdom and her experience as I will be again and as **you will be too**.*

So, if you are currently going through something that is shifting your world, that is changing everything or that feels deeply uncomfortable…

KNOW that you CAN move through it and you won't always know how it is meant to serve you but at some point in your life it will.

The path has been determined and you will find your way and the reason always reveals itself.

And also know that this will change you and that's okay. We are meant to change. And you are meant to share that change with the world.

I questioned everything in my life and the actions that I was taking in the last two weeks.

What is still relevant?
What am I wasting time and energy on?
What will I do next?
What do I truly want?

When life pushes you (and it will), use the opportunity to assess it all and make the necessary changes to live the life that you want most.

This young man, who passed on, was one of the BRIGHTEST lights I have ever known. He was unlike anyone I have ever met. He shone bright. He knew what he wanted even at his young age, he had a plan (a solid one) and he showed up daily being who he was meant to be. He knew who he was.

I encourage you to do the same.

It's time to rise.
It's time to SHINE BRIGHTER.
It's time to stop stopping.
It's time to be you.

If you are going through something hard right now, or if a hard time comes, you are exactly where you need to be and all you need to do is to continue to move forward one step at a time.

The universe always has your back.

. . . .

The next week passed very quickly. It was filled with many visits to his hometown, sleepless nights, so many more tears, hours of talking, supporting and encouraging words and of course the funeral.

I made a conscious decision to sit down again and document what I was feeling and experiencing. The following are my thoughts when I had that space to reflect and write about what we were going through.

A week later, I still believe that we are here to shine but what do you do when you don't know what that looks like?

> *When what was once relevant is no longer relevant.*

> *When what once mattered, doesn't seem to matter now.*

> *When you don't even know what you want anymore because you've let everyone else decide for you over and over again.*

How do you shine when you don't know who you are?

Well, you have to figure out who you are and what's next for you.

Who you are, depending on your experience of loss, could be radically different than who you once were.

It's hard to accept that. It's hard to maneuver in that. It's easier to hide.

Right now, watching my daughter grieve the loss of her

best friend, I'm questioning everything about the way this world works, why it is so hard and how I feel about all parts of my life.

I have had to accept the reality that my daughter won't be the same girl she was before the accident. I won't be the same mom or woman either. Watching her grief and her pain has created a shift in me as well.

So, how do you move forward?

I really just want to hide under my bed or lay on the couch or do the busywork and numb out.

But, I know from experience, that numbing out (with TV, social media, alcohol, shopping, menial tasks), isn't actually the way or the answer.

But how do you find the answer?

You have to ask yourself:

> "What do I want my legacy to be?"

> "What do I want now?"

> "How am I going to create meaning today?"

And then listen. Listen to the call of your soul.

You may not get the whole answer but you may hear the next step.

And then, it's up to you to take it.

. . . .

That first email that I wrote and the thoughts one week after my daughter's loss that you've just read spurred me on to write even more and to compile all that I have experienced over the last 18 years. It is what I have learned through a divorce, the death of my baby, a prolonged illness and now, walking my daughter through the loss of her best friend.

May it serve you and help you to see and explore the possibility of what can be next for you. My hope is that it will assist you in moving through your experience of loss feeling more understood, supported and universally loved.

And may it shine some light at the end of your tunnel to help you see the way out of the void.

1

When LOSS happens

After a loss, the world doesn't feel the same.

There is an emptiness that resides within you. There is a feeling of "who the hell cares anyways".

There is a lack of emotion and void that is almost indescribable.

My deepest journey into the void was when my baby died in June of 2006.

I wrote her birth story many years ago and it has been sitting on my desktop waiting for its place and it has finally found a home here.

June 14th, 2006 (6 something in the morning)

I was headed to the hospital to deliver our baby with my husband. Well, before we could get fully en route, my husband needed to stop and grab a coffee of course. His love of coffee superseded my labor pain apparently…I digress (and for the record, I did agree that he could stop because who knew how long of a day it would be for us).

At 38 ½ weeks, I was in labor with my second child and looking very forward to meeting this soul we had waited for these past nine months. The one who had created endless hours of morning sickness (in fact all day sickness for 5 months), joy in shopping for the cutest little clothes, and excitement (and some nerves) over what day he or she would make their appearance into this world.

My husband worked away from home the majority of each month so were hoping that he would make it home for the birth. He had arrived the day before. We were thrilled that he had made it. The timing had worked out and it was a big relief. My mom had arrived as well to take care of our oldest daughter. Everything was falling into place. No need to worry anymore. We were ready.

The drive to the hospital was quite uneventful. While I had labored at home since just after midnight, the contractions were still quite a few minutes apart and very manageable. We started out early because we wanted to beat rush hour traffic.

Upon arriving at the hospital at about 6:30, I was placed in the assessment room in labor and delivery and my husband went down to the registration desk to fill out the paperwork for my admittance to the hospital.

The nurses strapped the heart beat monitor on my belly for the baby and for some reason they were struggling to get the baby's heart beat and kept picking up mine. While the nurses remained professional and calm, I knew that when the third nurse came in to try to find the heartbeat, that there was a problem. For those of you that haven't had any children, when you are in the final stages of your pregnancy, the baby's heartbeat is super easy for them to pick up on; no searching for it is usually required.

When my husband returned back to the room, I filled him in on the struggle they were having to find the baby's heartbeat. The nurses told me that they called for the doctor on the team to come in and she would be arriving from her home shortly.

I knew it wasn't good.

I'm not certain that my husband quite understood what was truly happening but I already knew. I could tell by the nurse's reaction, underlying emotion and the urgency in which everyone was reacting. There was this façade of calm that overlay a feeling of panic.

Within 15 minutes of arriving at the hospital, I realized that the delivery and birth of our child would not be the joyous event we had hoped for. Our baby had died before we reached the hospital.

When the doctor arrived (which seemed like forever but was actually very timely), she confirmed with an ultrasound, that the baby's heart was not beating. She kept murmuring to herself and the monitor *"come on baby, come on heart, come on baby, come on heart"* and then she looked up at us.

The look on her face will be forever etched in my memory. Once the words, "I'm sorry…" left her lips, I was forever changed.

My life would never feel or be the same.

The grief was instantly overwhelming as were the many decisions that we needed to make. When the doctor told us that our child's heart was no longer beating, I remember hearing the horrible sound that was coming out my mouth. It felt as though I was watching myself cry and trying to make sense out of what was happening. It was surreal; almost an out-of-body experience.

Throughout that day, as we tried to accept what had happened, my husband and I spent a lot of time talking. I remember both of us repeating over and over that we needed to keep *moving forward* in our lives even though our baby had died.

I think we repeated it over and over again so that this commitment to **continue to live** would carry us through the grief and the unknown of what was to come for us.

We knew that we wouldn't move on, we would never forget the experience and we would never forget how much she impacted our lives. But, we would move forward and figure out how to live even though our lives had been drastically changed. My husband and I really knew and understood, even only hours after finding out that she had died and before I even delivered her, that **this child did not die for our lives to end**.

Even in our sorrow and through our many, many tears, it was with great clarity that we accepted this to be our new path.

Upon reflection, the day that my daughter died is the day that I began to understand what LIVING was really about.

There is no greater gift that Kassidy Quinn (our beautiful little girl) could have given to me on that day. It would take me some time to really understand this gift though.

Her death changed me in a way that would not have happened if she would have lived. I know that for sure. Now, I am truly grateful for the lesson about living more fully that she taught me on that day and the days that followed.

After finding out that my baby had died, they began prepping me for what lay ahead. I flat out refused to deliver the baby. I wanted a C-section. They kept telling me that it wasn't a good idea. I just couldn't wrap my head around delivering a dead baby. It made me so uncomfortable. What would that be like? How would I respond? What happens when you deliver the baby? How am I going to handle the pain of labor knowing that the end result isn't a baby that will cry when it is born?

It was SO MUCH to take in.

Once we found out her heart was no longer beating, they moved us to a different room away from all of the other women in labor. They had two rooms in a separate corridor for situations like the one we were in. I didn't realize where they had taken us at the time. I didn't even look around until we left at midnight that night and saw how secluded we actually were.

In fact, I don't even remember the transition from one room to the next. Did I walk? Was I in a wheelchair? I don't even know. What I do remember vividly though is hearing one woman screaming in labor pains (really carrying on) and just wanting to go and tell her to get it under control because at least her baby was alive. They moved me very quickly as her screams kept getting louder.

By this point, I had already called my parents and my mom was en route to the hospital. She had been dropping off our oldest at school just as we were finding out about the loss of our second child. In fact, while we were waiting for the doctor to arrive for the ultrasound, my mom phoned because she was unsure of what exit to take off of the freeway as she had never driven that route to school by herself. So as not to alarm her, we didn't say anything about the situation we knew we were about to face.

Once she had dropped our oldest daughter off at school, we called her back and she came to the hospital straight away. My dad, who was 8 hours away, left his tractor in the field and went to town to pack a bag and make the trip to our home.

When we got to the room and "settled in", my doctor arrived. Where I lived, doctors work in delivery teams so while you have a specific doctor throughout your pregnancy, you may or may not have your doctor at the hospital for the delivery. They had called my personal doctor though when they found out that the baby had died and he came to the hospital to consult and be with us.

He walked into the room with tears in his eyes. In fact, every nurse and caregiver that day did the same and expressed their sympathy. I know that the baby dying really impacted me but I also know that it impacted each of them as well. They had and would walk parents through this again in their careers many times.

When I was first pregnant, I was new to the city so I had to choose a doctor to monitor my pregnancy. Like pretty much everything else, my priorities for finding a doctor was based on their ability, any reviews I could find online and most importantly proximity to my home.

To be honest, my new doctor drove me crazy at the beginning of my pregnancy because he kept saying we were on a team together. A team? I don't think so. My husband participated in the getting pregnant part, the doctor was doing prenatal care and I was doing the rest of the work and I'm pretty sure neither of them felt like puking all of the time. I would scoff at his use of the word "team". (Never to his face though of course.) Some of my irritation likely stemmed from the fact that this pregnancy was exhausting for me and so nausea-filled.

But, on that day, when my baby died, we were a team. My doctor really encouraged me to deliver naturally. He gently reminded me that my heart would carry this scar forever but I didn't need my body to have one as well that I would see on a daily basis if I chose a C-section.

He promised me that once they induced me (my labor had stopped when I was given the news that the baby had died), if I felt that I couldn't do it, couldn't deliver the baby, then he would perform a C-section. But, I must give it a try first.

In the end, he was right. The scar on my heart was all I needed to carry. A visual reminder, the scar of a C-section, would have made the days and years to come even harder.

My doctor was someone I truly needed on my team that day.

There were many others on the team as well. There were two nurses who never left the room (except for a quick lunch break) all day. We always had someone with us monitoring me or just sitting during the process quietly off to the side in case we needed them. It was amazing care.

My mom had now arrived, my husband started phoning our closest family and friends and I was about to be induced. I asked if I could shower first.

The shower has always been a place for me to collect my thoughts. It's a quiet place for me to think. I needed to find some solace as my thoughts and emotions were overwhelming as was my task ahead of still delivering my baby.

My mom helped me to the shower and stayed with me in the bathroom. I remember standing under the stream of water thinking about why this was happening. I know that everything happens for a reason but in that moment I couldn't find a reason for why my baby had died.

I clearly recall saying to my mom "I can accept that this has happened but it is hard to not know why. It would have been so much easier to understand if it (the death of my baby) had just come with a note about what I needed to learn and why this happened to me".

There is a reason, a lesson and an opportunity for growth in every experience and even in that moment full of shock and pain, I still believed it.

But, I wanted to know the reason right away. Why couldn't loss come with a note that explains it?

It is hard enough to deal with someone close to you dying, why do you need to figure why and how this experience should impact you?

I still think about that day and wonder if that 'note' that I desired would have actually made it any easier. Would it have helped me to understand more clearly in those moments of extreme grief why these things happen?

I'm not sure it would have.

I'm not sure I would have been able to see the bigger picture and understand how it would all unfold.

I still feel sad when I think about the child that I never knew beyond nine wonderful months of planning for her to be in our lives.

But, through that feeling of sadness, comes joy when I think about how much she impacted our lives. How passionate I am about living and how it is through her inspiration that I live my life to the fullest each day. Things that seemed so important before are miniscule in the grand scale of life now. I really try not to get caught up in petty experiences or things that don't serve me. I strive to see the best in every situation and everyone. I focus on fulfilling my purpose and being happy on a daily basis.

My baby was born by mid-afternoon. The doctor and nurses were total professionals and made it so comfortable for us. They remarked at how beautiful she was, how much curly black hair there was and how she had her dad's ears. Once they had done some of what they needed to do, we were eager to see and hold her. Up to that moment, we didn't know how we would feel about seeing and holding her but they truly made it a really special experience for us with their enthusiasm. They cooed over her like she was living and breathing.

She had the same lips and nose as her older sister and her sisters that would come after her and the little bit of hair that we saw under her knit cap was divine (raven black and so curly). She was still warm and really looked at peace. She was perfect in every way.

We each held her and took in as much of her as we could trying to remember all of the little details.

We spent less than an hour with her and then came the

next hardest part. Letting her go. There is lots of testing that happens when your baby is stillborn for both the baby and the mother and they needed to do some of it in a timely manner. Now, there are something called cuddle cots which allow you more time with your child who has died because they cool the babies so that their bodies don't breakdown as quickly. (Please donate for one in your area if you can and let me know if you do. They are truly a gift to families to give them more time to process what is happening and spend time with their child.)

It was time.

We had to let her go.

My husband placed her in the bassinet and they wheeled her away. We wouldn't see her again.

We sent a special blanket for her to be wrapped in and a hat that my grandmother had knit for her.

And then the next part began.

The part where there was no longer a baby. She was gone from us now in every physical way.

It was late afternoon and I knew that I wanted to go home that night. The team of doctors and nurses were aware of what I wanted and were very focused on doing everything they could to make that happen.

Our eldest daughter, who was 7 at the time, still had no idea what had happened and I wanted to be the one to tell her the next morning as soon as she awoke. She had been so excited to have a little brother or sister. We had spent the two previous weekends prepping the final details in the baby's room. She had picked out all of the blankets, towels, socks and bibs at the store (spending a lot of time to pick the cutest ones) and lovingly arranged them in adorable little wicker baskets in her new sister or brother's closet. I would find her in there folding and refolding them daily so that everything was perfect for the new baby. She was going to be devastated and I needed to be the one to hold her through it all.

I had some complications and a fever following the delivery, so the medical team worked hard to get me well enough to go home. The thought of having to spend a night in that room was too much to bear and I needed to go home and sort out what was next for us.

Just before midnight, my fever had gone down and they decided it was safe for me to leave the hospital. I don't remember packing up but I do remember standing waiting for the elevator. The doors opened and as we were about to get on, a new dad was getting off with a congratulatory balloon in his hand. The look that crossed his face when he saw us standing there with a box was one of shock. I just stared blankly back at him.

It was like time stopped.

I was going home with a box, not a baby.

There would be no balloons and no celebration. I had a few polaroid pictures, a medical bracelet, a teddy bear that they had placed beside my baby girl in the pictures so that I had a reference of how big she was, the hat that they put on her when she was born and a beautiful certificate with her footprints in silver.

Those little footprints have made a big impact on my life.

I don't remember the ride down and when I stepped off that elevator, the journey into the void had already begun. I felt empty. My world was not recognizable. I was numb. We barely spoke on the way home. There was nothing to say.

My parents were waiting for us at home. I hadn't seen my dad yet and my mom had left the hospital that afternoon before our daughter was born. My husband and I had decided that we would be the only ones there when our baby was delivered.

We talked with them for a little while and then went to bed, not because we thought we would sleep necessarily but because there was nothing else to do. As I lay there, I did something that surprised me then and even surprises me now writing this. My nightly ritual was to say *"thank you for all that is, all that was and all that is to come"*. I laid my head onto my pillow and I automatically said that to myself. It was oddly comforting. It was like I knew that in some way this would serve me eventually.

How did I begin to move through the loss and the void?

Very purposely. I faced it every day in every moment.

I got up the next day and every single day after that and got dressed, did my hair and put my makeup on. I didn't necessary want to or feel like it but I did it because I knew I had to keep living. We even had a little birthday celebration for my mom two days later. She didn't want or expect us to do it but I wanted to show my young daughter that even in your deepest grief, you can celebrate and that you must continue to purposely live. You must celebrate in life and death. And for the first (and last) time ever, we ate three-layered chocolate cake with loads of chocolate icing for breakfast the next day.

I knew I needed to walk my family (and myself) through this. And the only way to do it was to face it all each day as best I could.

The decisions continued that week and the heart breaking phone calls were completed. We had actually called the majority of our friends and family that day at the hospital because I didn't want to have to do that from home. It was something that I wanted to get over with. With each call, it got harder, not easier. When our number came up on call display on their phone, they were anticipating the excitement of a birth of our new baby but the call that they received was very different. It was filled with sadness.

There was a flurry of activity with all of the decisions, calls and flower deliveries and then it got quiet. Too quiet. Deafeningly quiet.

Everyone's life returned back to "normal" except ours it seemed. This is one of the **hardest things to accept** after a loss (any type of loss from a death to a divorce to a job loss to a disease).

At this point, the awkward stage begins. People were awkward about what to say and what not to say. The sad, puppy dog eyes that I got were beginning to really bother me. And some of those around me stopped sharing about what was going in their lives because of what had happened in mine. It got more lonely and even a few of my closest relationships became strained.

As the days and months went on, there were still lots of tear-filled moments and times when I needed to leave the mall or couldn't go see babies that would have been the same age as my baby. But, I made a point of moving and doing something every single day. And I knew at some point, I would begin to feel more again. I would experience some joy. I would laugh a little more each day.

I'm not going to lie, it took awhile to find out who I was now and what this next part of my life would look like.

I remember being out in public that first week and hating the fact that no one else was feeling the pain that I was feeling. I would watch people laughing and enjoying themselves and it would be gut wrenching. It was hard. It made me want to stay home but I knew that avoiding it would just mean that I was delaying it. I had to face it. So, I did. In small doses and then in bigger doses and then some days I would go out only to come home 10 minutes later. You did what you had to do to get through another day.

That whole summer, I didn't spend more than a couple hours alone. I'm not actually sure why that's how it all happened but I didn't like how quiet it was alone. While my husband was away working for two weeks, my parents would stay with me and when he was home, they would head back to their house 8 hours away. It became the regular schedule that nobody talked about but just happened automatically for a couple of months.

I wasn't falling apart or unable to care for myself, it just became our routine that someone was always around. For me, this was very different because I had always loved being alone and having time and space to myself.

We went to the lake that summer like we did every year. It is all a bit of a blur. I don't remember most of it. I have one memory from a very hot day and I was walking across the street from the beach. We had just got off the boat and were getting some lunch. I had my ball cap on and I was feeling very unattractive with my post-pregnancy body and no baby to even show for it. I remember thinking "*how did this end up being my life*", shrugged at myself and then continued to trudge along.

My life felt so heavy and I was trudging forward through each day until one day, I realized that I was no longer trudging as much as I had been. It all felt a little lighter.

When we were to return home from the lake that summer, I looked at my mom and said, "I have to do this alone". My oldest was starting second grade and I needed to get comfortable being by myself again when my husband was away.

It was the first time that I had spent any time really alone in months. It was hard and it was still too quiet but I knew that I needed to keep moving forward and this was the next step. So, I took it.

And then, slowly but surely....

The grief changed.

The void got less thick.

The awkwardness waned.

And the world seemed more appealing.

I will tell you though that even now (more than 11 years later) when I see kids the same age as my daughter would have been, it still makes me catch my breath. I wonder what would have been and what could have been. And then, I move on to the next thought because wondering doesn't change any of it.

Wondering creates suffering and misery.

And I surely don't need any more of that. I **choose** to not put my focus and my energy on what might have been.

I don't really know when I moved completely through the void. The darkness and the numbness slowly receded as I began to accept and create my new normal. I was different and so it took awhile to realize what that meant for my life.

I quit my corporate career on the day my baby died. I continued my study of Feng Shui and personal growth during the hours my oldest daughter was at school and I began to do some consulting work to keep my days busier.

I was still numb but not as numb. And there is still a teeny part of me that remains vulnerable even now.

This type of loss is carved into your being. It doesn't leave you. You have healed but you aren't quite whole.

I never realized that I would continue to feel the loss even now. It is certainly not as heavy, it is not as sad and it doesn't consume me anymore like it once had.

It is the scar on my heart that my doctor told me that I would carry and have for the rest of my life.

That fall, I became pregnant again and the fear quickly set in. What if it happens again? What if this baby dies too? I had a 'meltdown' in my living room with my parents about that and then I realized that if it happened again, if this baby died too, I would walk through it again.

I had done it once so I would be able to do it again.

This deep knowing of yourself is how the void and great loss changes you the most.

It makes you more resilient.
It makes you stronger.
It makes you realize the depth of your personal power.
It makes you understand more of who you are and what you are capable of.

As I reflect back, I realize that the grieving was definitely the hardest the first year but it took about two years for me to feel more like me again; to be comfortable with who I was, how the experience had shifted me and how my world had changed.

I wrote about my experience during that first year but it took 11 years to share it all in a bigger way. I've talked about it but not presented more of my story in this way before. This book was the next step. It was time to share what these losses meant for my life and what your loss will mean for yours.

2

First stop: The VOID

You are living your daily life.

Something unexpected happens.
Something big.
A significant loss.

It changes everything and how you view everything.
Nothing in your life is now the same because of your loss.

The meaning disappears when nothing is the same.

There is a gap in your life now.

And once there is a gap, there is the void.

The experience of the void is almost not explainable. No words can really describe what it is or how it feels. Those who have been there understand what I mean. You only know it once you arrive there or have been there for any period of time in your life.

It is deep.

It is dark.

It is hollow.

It is timeless.

It is a place with no air and no obvious way to get out.

It will consume you if you let it.

It sucks the color out of your life. Everything feels like a shade of gray.

Some call it "*the dark night of the soul*".

When your life feels meaningless and the void deepens within you, the only thing you can do is to **accept your reality and begin to create your life again.**

This is one of the **hardest things** in life to have to do.

You have been forced into an experience that you weren't prepared for and you are the only one who can CHOOSE what is next.

You are likely resistant and reluctant to choose what you want now because you desperately want to go back to what was.

Even if your life wasn't great before your loss, it seems better than the unknown that you are currently experiencing. You probably don't know what you want next because you didn't plan for this. You didn't expect this type of loss to happen to you. No one does.

This wasn't the way that it "should" be.

This wasn't the way that things were "supposed" to go.

This wasn't in the plan that you had made for your life or even if you didn't have a plan made, this still wasn't part of it.

The pain.
The grief.
The suffering.
The void.

You don't want any of it. And yet, you are stuck with it and stuck in it. The void is best friends with denial and it usually swoops in next.

You will have denial of what is happening.

Denial that this is your life now.
Denial that you have to decide what is next.
Denial that it is up to you to find a way out of the void.

The road of denial is one that can consume you and take you further into the void if you let it.

Denying the reality of what is prolongs your experience in the void.

Acceptance of what is, the loss that you just experienced, is only about accepting that it happened. Acceptance does not mean that you have to like it or be okay with it. Accepting it means that denial cannot exist.

Denial keeps you stuck.

When you are first in the void, you may feel like you cannot even see the way or the light. It's so dark and consuming. You may not even know how you will ever have the ability to rise. But, it is possible, trust me.
You will begin to see the light because there is always light.

The void is a place where you can rise and shine from in a way that you didn't even know was possible. This is the choice you must make.

3

When the MEANING disappears

You may have experienced a tragedy, an unexpected loss, a divorce, separation or break up, a job loss, an illness or something else that has created a radical, unexpected change in your life.

Something has happened in your life and now nothing is the same or feels the same and everything that was "normal" is no longer normal.

Your life feels meaningless now. It's not recognizable.

Following each life event, experience and big change, there is a period of unknown. This creates the gap. In the gap, the meaning in your life feels lost.

This is the VOID.

It is uncomfortable. It is numb and it is a bit scary.

I know the void. I have been there a few times.

I've experienced a bitter divorce and custody battle, the loss of one of my children, a debilitating illness and most recently, I have walked my daughter through the devastating loss of her best friend. These are life changing events. Each one broke my world wide open, created a gap in the flow of my life and made me question my life's meaning.

The feeling of the void is familiar each time that you experience it. The depth of it, how much time you spend there and how consuming it becomes is all based on what you are going through and how you are choosing to see it and deal with it.

After each loss in my life, I questioned what life was truly about.

I briefly lost some of my faith in the goodness of the universe and in what I was meant to do and who I was meant to be. When my baby died and when I had my health crisis, I was deep in the void. All of the meaning I had created in my life seemed to disappear.

These experiences changed my life. Everything shifted each time and who I was and what I wanted wasn't the same anymore.

The void is a space where there are a lot of things to question and not a lot of answers.

> Where do I go now?

> I want to go back to the way it was but I'm too different to go back.

> I don't know who I am anymore.

> I no longer belong.

> I didn't plan for this so I don't even know what to do next.

> I don't know if what I thought I wanted before this experience is what I want now.

> What is even important anymore?

This is how you know you are in the void.

Nothing seems to make sense anymore, you are not sure if you really care about anything and you don't know if you will again.

The most significant questions that arise in the void are

    WHO AM I NOW because of what I've been through?

    What is the MEANING of my LIFE now?

These are the two hardest questions to answer after your loss.

Your journey must begin to figure it all out again, discover your new normal and create new meaning in your life.

As you begin to answer these questions, who am I and what is the meaning in my life, you will find your way out of the void.

These answers are your exit strategy.

4

The
IMPLOSION

The loss has happened. Nothing is the same.

Your life feels like it is imploding.

And...it is.

(No one around you may be brave enough to say it but I know that this is how it feels and it's important to acknowledge what is.)

Your life has radically changed in some way. I'm not here to pat you on the back and tell you that it will be okay. I am here to help you face it. That is how you will make it okay.

Nothing changes until it is faced.

Your life is NOT the same and as much as you may want to or try to put the "pieces" back together in the SAME way, you cannot go back to how it was before.

Too much is different now.

You are forced to create a different life now (if you CHOOSE to move out of the void).

You are different, so it will be different.

Let me say that again...

You are different, so it will be different.

And that's okay.

It really is.

Take a deep breath and surrender to this knowing.

Accept that this is why you feel so uncomfortable. You are not the same person you were before.

Everything has radically changed and the meaning in your life has seemingly disappeared. There is a gap and you are in the void.

You may not feel like you even know who you are anymore. You have entered into the 'dark night of the soul' and the framework from which you operated your life is no longer there.

Your life as you knew it, no longer exists. It is no longer your current reality.

And when the framework from which you've been operating your life from is gone (and this disappears in an instant when you experience a great loss, tragedy, illness, divorce or significant life event), the void arrives.

The emptiness, the nothingness and the lack of answers for what is next is overwhelming. You probably never knew that feelings of nothing could be so consuming.

The void exists right now for you because the meaning and framework of your life has been stripped away with your loss.

What you knew your life to be is not accessible in the same way anymore. You are currently existing in the void.

The only way to move through the void is to begin to create meaning again.

And when you do that, and I know that it will be hard and

that you don't necessarily want too, the void begins to disappear and the darkness begins to lighten.

The void CANNOT exist when your life is filling with meaning.

The darkness gets consumed by the light.

5

Will you LIVE?

The death of a loved one or a significant loss of something in your life like your partnership, your marriage, your health or your job, requires you to consciously CHOOSE to keep really living your life in each moment.

It truly is the only way out of the void and back into the light.

> You need to **LIVE** like you never have before.

> You need to **LIVE** with deeper meaning.

> You need to commit to **LIVING** fully.

That important person in your life did not die, the relationship or job did not end, and your health did not fail so that you would stop living your life.

You may never really know for sure why your loss happened. This may, at some point, be revealed but know that you are right where you need to be. It's both an ending and a beginning for you.

When a significant loss happens, everything feels like it stops because the way your life was progressing is no longer relevant. Your dreams may no longer be clear. What you want is no longer the same.

When something ends, you will see it all (your life, your experience and what's next) differently.

Your perspective has been shifted and this requires a new way of being. The energy has changed. You are forever changed.

It forces you to live differently.

n be a gift or a curse.

Which will it be?

Well, that is up to you and what you choose it to be.

This experience happened in your life and something ended so that you would have to CHOOSE how you will CONTINUE TO LIVE.

The acceptance of this change in you and your life really helps you move through this journey of loss that you are on.

You are not the same anymore because of what happened.

This ending and loss you have experienced or are currently experiencing can and will actually create greater understanding of who you are and what you are capable of if you let it.

It all happened so that you would RISE, not so that you would fall.

I know that this may be very hard to accept but it is the truth; whether you want it to be or not.

Living your life, rising up, is the only way to move through the loss, the grief and the void.

And the commitment to living fully gives you the power to choose how it all unfolds from here.

I know that there is a desire to hide and to just wish for your old life back and to say "I'm not choosing something new because I didn't choose to have to go through this" but the reality is that you are here and the choice from here is yours and yours alone.

The sooner that you can even slightly accept that all of this happened for you to RISE or even if you can just allow it to be a little true, you will shift towards creating meaning in your life again.

The more determination and courage that you can muster to move through this, face it and rise, the more fully you will live this next part of your life.

Your life will become this gift that you didn't know it be.

You will BE in this world in a way that creates more impact, serves more people and honors what you have lost.

It will reveal more of who you are now and who you were always meant to be.

I know that this is not really what you wanted to hear. Facing it is hard. You may be searching for an easier way through all of this. You won't find that answer here but I encourage you to keep reading with an open heart.

I hope you understand that I know how much you want to go back to what it was like in your life before.

I know. You need to know that I know.

There is something here for you though that you need to

hear. It is something that will allow you to live more freely again.

Let's continue this journey of moving through it.

6

A perspective SHIFT

After each loss, regardless of what the experience was (the divorce, the death of my child, the illness), I got more and more tired of the useless conversations, the complaints, the stories and mostly the overload of bad excuses and the shallow living that people were doing.

For someone who wasn't very judgmental and really didn't care what others did if they were happy doing it, the judgment rose in me in a very big way when my world was imploding.

I wanted everyone to WAKE UP. It was even more painful to watch everyone else focus on what I declared to be pointless stuff.

(It's important to note that some people are very awake, so I am making a generalization here that does not apply to everyone.)

I felt a version of this same experience after each loss.

> What they were complaining about really didn't matter.

> What they felt was so hard was not even a drop in the bucket compared to what grief and great loss was.

> What they were focused on was not actually that important.

> What they spent time talking and gossiping about really didn't matter.

> And what they worried about was all something that could be figured out.

I wanted them...to stop complaining about trivial stuff.

I wanted them...to remember HOW SHORT LIFE ACTUALLY IS.

I wanted them...to realize how much time, energy and effort they were wasting.

I wanted them...to focus on the important stuff not the fires in front of them that they could jump over anyways if they just got the guts to do it or stopped talking about it long enough to take action.

I wanted them...to realize that they were the problem and they WERE THE ONLY SOLUTION.

I wanted them...to delve deeper.

I wanted them...to fulfill their purpose.

I wanted them...to be all they could be and create what they truly wanted in their life.

I wanted them...to WAKE UP.

I wanted them... to realize that if they don't feel happy, they aren't doing the right work or taking the right actions. They can change that and they should

They didn't have a money, time or energy problem. They had a priority problem.

I felt like they had a skewed focus of what it meant to live.

Why was this how I viewed the world every time after each loss?

I don't really know.

I just couldn't deal with the stuff that didn't matter in a big way. I now had a different perspective because of the experience I had just been through and it made me look at it all from a different vantage point.

With my losses, I had been forced through such a range of deep emotions and life-altering grief that it made everything else in comparison feel shallow. It was the exact same response each time I experienced a significant loss in my life at age 23, 29, 37 and 40 years.

My perspective of life and what was truly hard had shifted. When you go through a loss and experience the void, your perspective shifts.

You now have a different lens through which you look at your life and so how you see others changes as well.

Your view is very different from the one that most of those people around you are filtering their life through. Accepting their reality while trying to cope with what you've been through can be one of the hardest parts of the journey through loss.

I wanted to shout....

> Your life isn't that bad. Just choose to do something about it.
>
> Stop lying to yourself.
>
> You aren't focused on the stuff that matters most.

Stop complaining about it.

Change it.

This what I most wanted to say though:

> You don't have to experience what I am going
> through so that you understand how to live fully.

> Just begin by doing you and becoming who you were
> meant to be.

> You deserve more because you are more.

> You are here to live the life you want most.

After each loss, the sheer frustration I was filled with
about the world and those around me, was actually a great
gift for me.

It showed me what I wanted to make important in my life
moving forward and it gave me greater perspective into
who I wanted to be now.

In some ways, the anger, annoyance and judgment of
others gave me an outlet as well that helped me to
continue to walk through the void. It was a way to release
some of the emotion. A feeling of any emotion was better
than being numb. At some point after a loss, the tears
always dry up and the numbness settles in even further.

I thank those for what I judged in them and their life
because it made me realize what I wanted living my life to
really be like.

Once I moved through the void, I always went back to my
accepting self and supported others however they chose to

live their life. And all of those things that I wanted to say in those moments when I was in the void, never passed through my lips.

Truly, it's up to them.

And my life is up to me.

And your life is yours to live.

It can be whatever you want it to be. I truly believe that you should live the way that you want.

So, if you are in the void and you are feeling annoyance with the actions of the people around you, realize that this is normal and expected. Accept your emotions and accept that they get to choose their own life.

You've changed.

It's okay.

Your viewpoint has changed.

You have experienced a great loss and the gap in meaning in your life that happens in the void.

Your perspective has shifted.

This is the beginning of your new normal.

7

Your TITLE changes

Because you haven't already been through enough, how the world identifies you changes now as well.

You end up with a title that you didn't necessarily want or ever consider that you would take on in your life.

You are now a:

Widower.

Divorcee.

Cancer survivor

Mother of 4, Parent to 3

_____ (Fill in the blank with the title that society labels you with now.)

Maneuvering these titles can be hard. I used to hate checking that divorced box on forms. Not because I regretted my divorce but because of the stigma attached to it at that time.

When I get asked how many children I have, there are a couple thoughts I run through to decide how I will answer that question.

Do I say I have four kids or three?

Do I feel like sharing my story today?

And then, I think about how my girls will respond if they are with me when I am asked. Sometimes, when I say I have three children, one of my younger girls will interject and say "What about Kassidy?" and then I have to tell my story anyways.

Even after 11 years, I don't always know how to maneuver the title Mother of 4, Parent to 3. It's uncomfortable for me. It makes me feel a little twisted up inside. It wasn't (and still isn't) a title I wanted.

The title is just a label though.

The label only describes the experience.

It isn't who you are.

It just reveals some of your life experience to the world. And sometimes you don't necessarily want the world to know.

What do I do to deal with the new titles?

I tell my story when I want to and when I don't, I don't. Sometimes I'm open about my health issues, my divorce and my baby dying and sometimes I'm not.

I get to decide what I want to share.

Who you are and what you label in your life is always up to you.

Give yourself permission to tell whatever part of your life story that you want.

It's your story.

You get to decide what you want to share.

8

The lack of understanding is HARD

When you go through a significant loss and something that radically shifts your world, not everyone around you will understand the experience that you are having. They will pat you on the back, give you a hug and say a variation of one of these things:

>"The funeral will bring closure."

>"There is always a reason and a lesson."

>"You are only given challenges that you are capable of handling."

>"You have to move on."

>"There are worse things."

>"It must be karma."

And on and on. I'm sure you can add some to this list.

Is there truth to any of them? Maybe. Probably. Likely.

Does it matter to you right now? Not really.

Your experience is YOUR experience.

While I know some of what you are going through if we've had similar life events happen, I don't know your experience. I do not know why this happened to you nor do I have the perfect answer for how to help you walk you through it.

I don't know. And no one else knows either.

When a loss happens, there can be a lot of advice shared from those who don't really know or haven't been through something similar.

People are desperate to make you feel better and so they sometimes say too much or not enough. A lot of the time, people just don't know what to say. It's hard to know what to say to someone because there are usually very few words that can actually provide comfort and take some of the pain away.

In each of my experiences, I turned to and listened to people who had actually gone through a divorce and a long custody battle, to the mothers who had lost babies and to people with auto-immune diseases and adrenal fatigue.

I sought advice, solace and support from those who had a similar experience as mine because I knew that they understood more of what I was going through.

They were relatable.

They knew the void.

They knew the depth of the loss.

They knew the road to recovering from it all.

They knew.

I know too. I know it from my experience but not from yours.

Seek out people who have been through similar experiences and who have recreated their lives. They will understand you and where you are at in a deeper way.

I sought out those whose babies had been born silently

that were full term because they knew what it is was like to have to deliver a child who was not alive. They knew what it was like to look at a baby who appeared to be sleeping but wasn't breathing. They knew what it was like to walk into that empty nursery that we had so lovingly put together in our home and face the fact that the baby would not lie in that crib. They knew the pain of having to decide what to do with the things she would never use and then pack them away. They knew what is was like for my milk to come in but no baby there to feed. They knew.

Seek out people who know.

They will help you move through this. They will help you discover who you will become now in all of this. And they will give you hope that the sun will shine more brightly in your world again because they have done it.

Receive the love and support and the words that are meant to be kind from all of those around you and use them to fuel you. Don't worry too much about what they are saying or aren't saying if it doesn't feel right to you. Just focus on the fact that they are wanting to love and support you.

Be gracious with all of those who may not have used the "right" words. They are doing the best that they can with what they know and what they have experienced. Just as you are doing right now too.

If you are reading this and want to know what to do when someone close to you is experiencing a great loss, this is what I've learned:

The most comfort you can provide is by spending time

with them, showering them with love and being there for them not just after it happens but for the months that it will take for them to even begin to process it and feel like they are living again.

There are probably few words that you can say that will actually take their pain away. Spend your time listening when they are wanting to talk. Let them share. It's okay to acknowledge that you don't know exactly what to say or do. Ask them what they need right now and if they don't know, just love them. Please don't decide how their journey through this should go, just walk with them through it.

9

The
BEFORE
and
the AFTER

Your world, your life, and your experience is now divided into two:

BEFORE and AFTER.

Before you got sick.
Before your child died.
Before the divorce.
Before the job.

After the illness.
After the loss.
After the divorce.
After the job.

Your life now has this odd delineation of before and after. And because of this, when you speak about your life, you will talk of times before your loss and then you will talk about the 'after'.

For some, this before and after experience creates a new chapter in your life but for most, it is like writing a whole new book. Because of your loss, the book of "before" is complete and the book of "after" is just beginning.

The book of 'after', the new story, is one that you begin creating from the void with every step you take towards the light.

I think about before my divorce and how my dream was the white picket fence, the two kids and the happily ever after and then I found myself having to check the divorce box on the government forms and explain why my child had a different last name.

Before the illness, I didn't even realize how lucky I was or how healthy I had been and how much easier life was when you can move freely, drive wherever you want and jump on an airplane with ease. There are days when I'm so thrilled that I am feeling good and have been able to do all of the errands and then still take the girls to their activities without any side effects of my illness and any discomfort. Whereas before the illness, I never would have even thought about how lucky I was that my body could handle all of those activities in one day.

I used to only worry about getting through the first trimester of a pregnancy and had never considered anything going terribly wrong at the end. After my baby died, I felt more uneasy and apprehensive the whole way through the next two pregnancies. The discomfort and fear elevated even more as I neared the end of each pregnancy.

The story of my 'after' with my baby being stillborn meant that I didn't get excited about my next two children while I was pregnant with them in case they didn't live. I couldn't let myself be that vulnerable. I withheld my excitement. I felt like I held my breath the whole 9 months until my daughters were born alive and placed in my arms. That is the moment when I began to celebrate and enjoy them.

As for my oldest daughter, I know that she is no longer as innocent as she once was, she has felt deep grief from the loss of someone so close to her. How does this impact her now? Time will only tell how this changes her experience in this new story of her 'after'.

It is hard when you compare the before and after when the loss is still new. It does get easier as you get further away from the "before" but that division will always be there now. It remains a part of your life story.

No matter how much you embrace your new normal, your life is now defined with a before and an after.

The key is to find the joy in both.

Focus on that.

There is goodness in both if you look hard enough and dig deep enough.

I know that all of my losses have made me a better person, a more aware soul and a freer being.

To begin with, you will just exist in the after. The after is awkward, unfamiliar, filled with resistance and all very new.

The before is made up of memories.

You are now living in the after.

It's time to begin creating meaning in this part of your life story.

10

The
WAY

What you are experiencing doesn't feel fair.
What you are experiencing feels like hell on earth.
What you are experiencing feels brutal.

I understand how you are feeling.

I am here to remind you that there is a way through this, there is a way to create meaning again and there is a way to move through the darkness and the void.

I am here to give you hope.

Hope is the way to the light.

Hope is the first step in trusting that it will begin to feel better again.

Hope reveals and reinstates some meaning in your life.

What you are going through is very hard and it will continue to be hard if you don't start creating some meaning (even a teeny bit of it) every day.

You have to counteract how hard going through this experience is with some meaning.

The joy that you experienced with the person, in the marriage or at the job must always override the current pain of the loss.

Don't let the loss overshadow what was good. Don't let the loss become the most thought about part of the whole experience.

This is what my dad said to me when I arrived home from

the hospital after my baby had died. I remember exactly where he was sitting in my living room and exactly what he said. I had only talked to him that morning to tell him that the baby had died and then I didn't speak to him again until midnight when we got home. He looked at me from across the room and said "the loss can't be bigger than the joy you experienced in preparing for her".

This one statement helped me face the loss and move through the void in a very significant way.

And even now, when I'm sad about it or when I was going through the other experiences of significant loss in my life or just hard life events, I remember to make the joy bigger than the grief.

The joy must always outweigh the grief.

I told this to my oldest daughter right after we found out that her beloved friend had died.

I first though, held her face in my hands, as she was crumbled on the floor, and said to her "that I was so sorry that she was going to have to go through this and this was now a part of her life experience".

I really was .

My heart ached for her heart.

I also told her that I didn't know why this happened but she must find a way to accept it.

I knew that there was no way for me or anyone else to take her pain away. The only way for the pain to lessen was to keep moving through it and to face it. As her mom, I shed many tears knowing that I could walk with her through this but only she could find a way to heal from the pain. I couldn't heal it for her.

That knowing was one of the most difficult parts of watching my daughter lose her best friend. I could and did share every piece of wisdom I had with her, but only she could choose how she was going to get through this and how it would change her life.

Over the next few weeks, I kept repeating to her "don't let the loss of him be bigger than the joy and the good times that you shared with him". I said it over and over and over again to her hoping that it would help her like it helped me. It was the one statement that carried me through the void and into the light again when my baby died. The grief must not outweigh the joy.

If I had let the grief overshadow the joy, I wouldn't have honored the life that my baby did have and I wouldn't have been honoring the life that I still had yet to live.

The loss and the experience you are going through can't overshadow the joy.

Don't let it.

You are in charge of that.

The grief that one experiences after a loss (any loss) is mainly for the things in the future that won't and can't happen now.

The joy is experienced based on what we remember and what we enjoyed about the person, the marriage, our health or the job. The grief that is based on this future thinking is not even real and yet it can consume you. It is all you can focus on and it only feels empty.

Can you imagine how it would change your experience in the process of a death, a divorce, a loss of a job or an illness if you focused on not letting the grief outweigh the joy? What if you held the joy in high regard and did not grieve a future that didn't exist to begin with?

This one thing can change how you feel about it and how you walk through your loss and the void.

Grief is amplified when we focus on what we think we are missing in the future.

Are we missing something? Do we glorify what some of it might be? Is it normal to focus on what might have been?

Yes to all of these things.

But, when one recognizes and faces the fact that the future creates a lot of the grief, one can start seeing the light in the present moment again.

Remember that you are not alone in the experience of grief and the void.

Look around.

There are many people surrounding you that are experiencing what you are experiencing. We are interconnected.

There are many who have stayed in the void and then there are those, like you and me, who choose to RISE; to not be overcome by the loss but to use the loss to add more value to the world and to create a bigger impact because of the experience.

It will not be easy. But, it is possible.

And this possibility is fueled by the hope that you need to trust yourself, others and the world again.

What you are going or have gone through is not meaningless. It is probably the most meaningful thing that will ever happen to you because it changed your life.

It has revealed who you are and what you are made of.

You will find a way through this.

You already are.

11

Letting go of the WHY

The unanswerable question....

WHY?

I don't know WHY you are going through this. I wish I could answer that for you. It would take away so much of the pain from the loss and ease your grieving process.

I never knew WHY I was going through any of it either.

I now finally understand some of WHY I went through the loss of my baby.

Why is my once vibrant, fun loving, beautiful teenager experiencing a tragic loss? I don't know. Not having this answer for my oldest daughter, as the one she looks to for answers, is so hard.

The not knowing why it happened to you is one of the hardest parts of any loss.

You are in a position where you have to accept that it has happened and your new reality without truly knowing WHY you are experiencing it.

You must accept that you may never know fully why. This may always be an unanswerable question in your life.

We constantly search for answers. We are wired that way.

And in most situations, no matter who you try to blame, no matter how much you think it through and no matter how much you "what if" it, you likely won't come to an answer that satisfies WHY this has or is happening to you.

Some call it fate, some say it is destiny, some proclaim

that it is karma. That provides an "answer" but is it one that makes you feel better? Only you can decide that.

The wondering WHY it happened will suck you dry even more on a daily basis. It literally drains you. It keeps you in the void.

You won't know any part of the WHY until you need to know. And then more of it will make "sense".

It seems like a nasty game the universe plays on us. You experience a loss. Your whole life shifts and you don't get to necessarily know why this is happening to you right away or ever at all. Yet, you have to find a way to deal with the loss and accept that you don't know WHY.

When my baby died, I wanted a note that told me what I needed to learn and what the lesson was in this experience for me and why I needed to go through this in my life. Well, my note and my reason WHY arrived over 11 years later.

I get it now. Some more of the reason why my baby died was finally revealed.

What did this revelation do for me?

It made me realize that the pain and the grief that I experienced wasn't for naught. It doesn't make it better or easier to not have her with me but I know how much it changed me and I know why I needed it to change me. It gave me a depth of understanding and knowledge that I didn't know I had or even needed until my oldest daughter was grieving.

Here's the truth (or at least, what I feel is true)...

You have to let go of trying to figure out why it happened.

You have to let go of the guilt of your role (if you had one or not).

You have to let go of what you did or didn't say.

You have to let go of the need to UNDERSTAND.

All of this will hold you back. All of this is holding you back.

It will keep you in the void or keep sucking you back in.

It will keep you stuck in the past.

You will not find meaning when you seek to understand something that is not understandable; there may never be an answer that will make it feel okay.

You have to accept the reality of what is. And when you do this, the light will brighten.

This is hard.

I'm not going to say it is easy because knowing "why" would likely be easier than not knowing in most cases.

We found out how my baby died. She had a knot in her umbilical cord that got pulled tight during labor. They had actually prepared us for not knowing how or why she died because in a lot of cases they don't know how the baby died. That knot would have been formed in the first trimester and she went through the second and most of the third trimester with it, with no issues. It didn't impact her until labor began (only 1 in 2000 babies die from this). So, the 'how' of why she died was explained but it didn't create any comfort or answer the questions "Why is this happening to me?" and "Why is this my life experience?"

The reality is that it happened.

The reality is that I had to deal with it.

The reality is that you must deal with your loss.

At some point, you must reach a level of acceptance.

You will never move on from this experience of loss in your life because it is engrained in your being and in your heart. But, you can move forward and move through it and that is what you are being called to do.

That is why you are here.
You can do this.
I know it.
Because I've done it.

Find a way.

Release the need to know why.

Surrender to the reality of what is.

12

KNOW this

Know that you are loved.

Know that you are understood in this space.

Know that you can rise again.

Know that you are powerful and can choose how to move through this experience and it can make you even stronger.

I see you.
I see your pain.
I acknowledge your pain.
And I am here to give you a glimmer of hope and a slice of light.

I am here to help you RISE. What will it take?

> It takes a COMMITMENT TO LIVE.

> It takes a desire to fulfill the call of your soul.

> It takes faith, hope and a lot of trust.

> It takes the deep inner knowing that you can do this (because you can).

> It takes perseverance and commitment.

This is likely one of the hardest things you will ever do. And it will be worth it. Believe me. I know it to be true.

You have to promise yourself that you can do this and you will do this. This commitment will guide and carry you through.

How do I know that you can do this?

Because you are reading this now.

Because you have sought out some answers and because you are ready to continue to move through this.

Because you can. We all can.

The void has held some of the greatest teaching moments of my life each time I've walked through it.

The void really shows you how much everything actually means in your life.

It separates what you thought was important from what is actually important.

I know more about myself because of it. I know more of what I want. I know more of what was distracting me that will never distract me again like petty gossip, empty conversations, strained friendships....all were gone after the death of my baby.

You will experience the same thing. You will learn more about who you are, what you want and what you do not want in your life anymore because of your loss.

There is a lot of wondering and questioning that happens when you experience a great loss.

How can I trust again?
How can I love again?
How can I be vulnerable again?

How can I enjoy life again?

You can and you will. With time.

But you won't do it in the same way you did before because you are different and that's exactly the way it should be.

Accept what is.
Be as open as you can be.

Know that you can begin to live again.

Know that your heart will feel lighter when you do.

13

The
GIFT

Just over a year after my baby died, in September of 2007, I was shopping after the birth of my third daughter (my rainbow baby). We were in the grocery store, she was in her car seat in the cart and I had quickly found what I needed and was in line to pay for my items.

The line that I chose to wait to pay for my groceries was at a standstill as they were doing a price check, so I chose a different line that only had three people in front of me. My daughter was sleeping soundly at that point but if she woke up, the whole store would know how much of a screamer she was.

When it was my turn to pay for my items, the cashier (a women in her early 30s) rang them through but didn't tell me my total which I thought was odd. So, I looked at the screen and started getting the money out of my wallet to pay for the groceries.

I went to hand the money to the cashier and realized that she was shaking, crying and couldn't stop staring at my baby. In slight shock at the experience that was happening, I asked her if she was okay. She was so upset that she couldn't even speak. Finally, I grabbed her arm, got her to look at me and asked her again if she was okay.

She shook her head and through her sobs told me that her baby had just died a couple of weeks ago and this was her first shift back at work. Her baby would have been the same age as my daughter who was peacefully sleeping in her car seat. She started apologizing profusely for getting so upset.

At that point, one of her co-workers had come over to help console her. Because the cashier kept apologizing to me and was embarrassed at her emotional outburst, I told her that I had gone through the same thing. It wasn't something that I had shared openly with people I didn't know up until that point. It was still too emotional for me to share a lot about it. I asked her if she had a boy or a girl and what she named her baby. She had given birth to a boy.

Sometimes people think that because the baby dies silently that it is easier not to acknowledge the birth – this can be even harder on the parents than you expressing your sympathy (even if it is awkward) about the death. I knew the importance of finding out some of the details about her baby. It would always be her first born.

I asked what color hair he had and how far along she was when he died (she was very close to her due date). Her co-worker was quick to point out that I already had a new baby and that she could try again when she was ready and her next baby would be fine like mine had been.

The cashier kept repeating that she didn't know what she did wrong and what she could have changed so that it wouldn't have happened. I reassured her that she did nothing wrong and that her baby wasn't ready to be in this world. I asked what her favorite part of the pregnancy was and encouraged her to focus on the joy she felt as she prepared for the arrival of the baby throughout the pregnancy. These are the actual experiences that happen in our lives, not the future ones that we create in our minds that we tend to grieve the most about.

Our grief increases and becomes even more overwhelming because we focus on what could have happened and what might have been.

I gently told her that her baby didn't die for her life to come to a standstill and that her baby would want her to keep living her fullest life.

Sometimes, in the depth of grief, we forget to give ourselves permission to live.

After almost 10 minutes of steady talking with these women, it was time for me to go. I only hoped that I had provided some solace and hope to this young woman. I have always wondered if she decided to have another baby after her loss. It takes a lot of courage and faith to choose to become pregnant again.

I left the store, got in my truck, called my mother and burst into tears. I was so upset and felt terrible that this woman believed that it was her fault and that she could have done something to make the death not happen. Throughout my experience of losing my baby, I had never once even considered that it was my fault. I even had labor contractions, over the course of about five hours, a few days prior to losing my baby. Because they weren't consistent and not very strong, I didn't go in to the hospital. Had I chose to, my baby may have lived. I don't know that for sure and on that day, my contractions stopped so there was no reason to think that I had made the "wrong" choice. I don't reflect on that and blame myself like the young cashier was blaming herself for her loss.

She was in the VOID.

She was searching for meaning and not really ready to be

back at work but not knowing what else to do. She was having to continue on even though her whole world had been shattered by this loss. When the people around you aren't in the void and maybe never have been, it is even more lonely. It is suffocating and it is a life changer.

I knew that feeling.

I knew that void.

I knew how hard it was to continue to move.

But moving is the only way through. Otherwise, you just stay stuck in the void.

As the light grows brighter, you are somewhere new. You don't go back. Nothing is ever the same.

Once you have moved through the void, every single thing holds so much more meaning. The void brings such clarity about what is truly important to you and what matters most.

This is the gift.

The hard part is that one must first experience the void to understand what living your life really means.

It was on that day, after meeting the women who was working in the grocery store, that I decided to to write even more of my story.

The journey through the loss of my baby and the process of grieving ebbed and flowed over the course of the next year or so. Even now, over 11 years later, I can tear up thinking about it and be transported back to that day in an instant. I think, in fact I know, that is why it has taken me so long to write my story.

My baby dying changed me.

It made me a better person.

It shifted my perspective.

It changed how I did everything.

It served me and made me who I am now.

It made my life more meaningful.

When it first happened, I would never have known that this is what I would eventually feel.

I didn't realize the gift that I had been given.

I appreciate my life so much more now. But, after the loss, it was a journey to get to this place of peace.

I know you can do it too. If you choose too.

14

Another VISIT to the void

Fast forward a couple of years when a different type of loss and life experience would create a gap and an entry into the void again.

By now, I had delivered my fourth child and my life was very full being a mom of 3 girls and doing some consulting work when I could find some time.

During the end of 2012, my health, well-being and vibrancy was fading rapidly and the journey into the void had begun. I could feel it happening and there seemed to be nothing that I could do to stop it.

It all started with some slight fatigue and uncomfortable responses to food (no food in particular but the allergic reactions were becoming more noticeable and more frequent). The degradation of my health continued and I struggled with my vision at night, then the fatigue increased and the food issues got worse. I went to my Chinese Medicine Doctor and we worked together for about 9 months. I had regular acupuncture appointments and the symptoms seemed to be improving somewhat but I was still struggling with exhaustion. I was trying everything from changing my diet to sleeping even more to trying new workouts. Nothing seemed to really help.

As per usual, we spent a lot of the summer at the lake. I would grab my lawn chair, find a nice spot of beach and watch the girls (who were 4, 6 and 14 at the time) play in the water everyday for hours. I got some extra help from my mom and dad with the girlies, an opportunity for a little personal space and a welcome change of pace from our life in the city during my lake time. We certainly look forward to our beach days every year.

When I returned back home in late August in preparation for getting the girls back to school and starting all of their extra curricular activities, the great fatigue really began to settle in. I was tired ALL of the time not just in the mornings and late afternoon anymore.

By Christmas, it was all I could do to get out of bed in the morning and get the kids to school to then lay on the couch until I had to pick them up again. Beyond a weekly trip to the grocery store, making meals and keeping up with the laundry, laying on the couch was pretty much what I did all day. I didn't even have enough energy to watch TV let alone stay awake during a show. I wasn't well enough to attend my girl's activities and didn't even go to the Christmas concerts that year. My husband went to all of the events that he could for the girls when he was home and my eldest daughter filled my role at the other activities for my littler girls.

The big health scare happened at the end of February 2014. I ate something that I had made many times before and it was made from "scratch" (all homemade and all 'clean' ingredients). We were gluten, dairy and sugar-free at that point and had been for years. Shortly after supper, I began having a significant allergic reaction.

It became so strained to breathe that I knew it wasn't safe for me to be at home with my girls. I called one of our close friends to take me to the hospital. Upon arrival, they monitored me as I was experiencing the allergic reaction and then quite a few hours later, sent me home once I was breathing easier again. The doctor suggested that I take an antihistamine before each meal to avoid any further reactions, as the tests had been inconclusive. That really didn't feel like a sustainable solution, so it was time to do even more to determine what was happening and find a better solution than popping an antihistamine so that I could eat comfortably.

A couple of months prior to the soup-inducing allergy attack, I had found out about a Functional Medicine Doctor in the city where I lived but I had resisted the idea of going as it was very expensive and I had convinced myself that maybe I just wasn't sick enough to warrant it.

Well, now I was.

My husband and I decided that there was no other option. My health was of course more important than the money so it was time to make the investment and book the appointment. I needed to get to the root cause of my ailing health and a Functional Medicine approach would provide that for me hopefully.

After copious amounts of blood work and other testing (my bathroom counter looked like a lab experiment for a few weeks), the Functional Medicine Doctor ruled out Lyme Disease and one other disease that I had never heard of before (I had so much brain fog at that point that I never did remember the name of it).

In the end, I was diagnosed with Stage 3 adrenal fatigue. Basically, I had totally burnt out my adrenals and my body was depleting rapidly because of it. My hormones and vitamin levels had dwindled to a very depleted state and my body was struggling to function.

I remember asking my doctor "how many stages are there?" I'm always the optimist, so I figured there must be at least 5 or 6 stages in his assessment scale.

His response: "3".

Hmmm, this might be a little worse than I'd like it to be.

Me: "Well, what's next then?"

Him: "If you want to get well, you need to quit your life for a year."

Me: "Pardon? Not possible. I have three kids and my husband works away."

Him: "I know. Keep them alive for a year. Take them to school and feed them. That's it. No other external pressure and no other tasks. Offload every single thing that you can. I want you to lay on the couch until you can sit in the chair comfortably and then maybe you can sit at your desk...."

Because I knew that I was out of options, I agreed and the treatment protocol got laid out and I did it.

I went ALL IN.

I went all in partly because I was so tired and laying on the couch was all I could do anyways so it was nice to have "permission" to do that but mainly because he told me that if I did this for a year, I would get better exponentially faster. I figured trading a year of my life was better than a slower progression of healing. I was sick and tired of being sick and tired.

During that year, my favorite word became NO.

I said no to everything and everyone. I said no to friends,

to my kids, to invites, to clients, to my parents, to people I didn't know. No, no, no.

Looking back, it was a powerful exercise in setting boundaries and a word that I still use to this day quite proficiently. Saying no declared to the universe (and to me) that this is my life and I am going to choose how I spend my time, my energy and my effort. The year on the couch really taught me how to consciously set boundaries.

Between all of the testing, the bio and neurofeedback and the numerous supplements (multiple handfuls five times per day), the strict diet and the structured daily schedule, my Functional Medicine Doctor also taught me the most vital part of recovery. **I needed to change everything of what I had done, how I had thought and who I was being** so that I wouldn't compromise my health again and end up back in his office in 5 years in worse health than I already was.

EVERYTHING HAD TO CHANGE.

I had to be different to create a different result.

And in fact, it had all changed already.

After a diagnosis and during the healing process, you are not the same person that you were before your health issue. You now appreciate things differently, you see things through a different viewpoint and your perspective of living has shifted.

You experience the void when your health challenges impact how you can live your life.

I didn't realize that a health crisis could create so much

grief and a gap in your world. You can enter the void slowly or be thrust into it right when a loss happens or when you receive a life altering diagnosis for your health.

What is meaningful in your life comes into question because sometimes you can no longer do the things that you could easily do prior to getting sick. Relationships change and some friendships even end because it's hard for them to see you sick. A lot of what was once so important in your life is no longer important because your perspective has changed

When something happens, like a health issue or scare, nothing is the same and you can slip into the void.

For me, the void deepened as I got sicker and became a 'shadow version' of myself. From the outside everything looked okay, not great but okay, but on the inside, I didn't feel well at all. It was a struggle to do anything. I didn't recognize who I was and I just didn't know what to do anymore. I felt empty and I lacked purpose. I didn't care about my work which was something that I had always loved and looked forward to spending time on when the girls were at school.

The void consumed me even more when I was unable to do the things that I had so easily done before like client consultations, team trainings, getting groceries or even getting up in the morning. I didn't recognize myself and couldn't figure out why this was happening to me.

Who had I become?

What had been important, wasn't important anymore. I didn't know if I would ever be the same again. I felt like an empty vessel, a shell. I felt a little like I was dying. I drained and I was withering away. The meaning I or had was gone. I was deep in the void.

I saw the first bit of light in this void when I finally got diagnosed and when there was a treatment plan in place.

Just like when someone close to you dies, when illness happens, you ask yourself those deeper questions. Those same questions I had asked in my first experience of the void when my baby died.

Why did this happen to me?

What does it mean for what I thought I wanted?

Does anything that I thought mattered, really matter?

What matters now?

Who am I now?

And then, the search for the answers begins. You might still be sick as you uncover who you are now or you may be recovering or healed when you figure it all out. As you determine more of what you want, what matters to you and who you are now, you begin to develop meaning again and you move out of the void.

I took the year off and laid on the couch for the vast majority of it. In the late winter, I had graduated to sitting in the chair for most of the day and I took an online course to fill the time I needed to still stay at the house. I might have been on "house arrest" but you could not stop me from learning, growing and finding a way to create meaning and live more fully.

The work that I did before I got sick included workshops, team meetings and individual appointments and at that stage in my recovery, it was unclear if I would be able to go back to the work I used to do with my clients in person.

My doctor knew that he could get me healthier but we didn't know how healthy I would become. Once you burn out your adrenals, they are usually never really the same again. They don't operate with the same capacity and are more sensitive to stressors and being drained than they once were.

I began to create my "new" normal which included taking an online course about putting your courses online (say that 5 times fast). I loved it. It helped me **create meaning in my life again**. It got me back to my work and that is something that feeds my soul, makes me feel alive and excites me about the possibilities of life.

While I have definitely exited from the void (that happened when I was ready to start learning again to take my business online), my healing journey continues.

15

Being forced to CHANGE

It was early 2017 and I was thinking that I had it all "figured out" and my life was finally beginning to flow again. My health was continuing to steadily improve with no major setbacks. My new online business approach was thriving and growing and I was enjoying the new rhythm and routine in my life. Unexpectedly, like it always usually is, the meaning in my life once again was questioned.

In March, my eldest daughter experienced the loss of her best friend. I watched the meaning in her life shatter. I watched her slip into the void. I saw the sadness in those once sparkly eyes. I witnessed her begin to walk through the emptiness of what had been a fun-filled life and try to decide what was meaningful now.

As I watched her, I wasn't totally sure what my life meant anymore either. I questioned the fairness of life. I wondered why a teenager would have to experience such grief especially at time when a big life event was about to happen with her graduation from high school. An event that every student looks forward to in their senior year.

And after graduation, her and her best friend were excited to be headed to the same university. They would finally be living in the same city and would see each other more. They were already making plans.

My faith in the world was shaken as I tried to understand why this devastating loss had to be a part of her life's journey.

I also began to wonder if what I was doing to add value to this world was even really meaningful at all.

These life events (deaths, divorces, health issues or

whatever it has been for you) FORCE us to change.

They are a period of major personal expansion and growth that is filled with pain.

It is very HARD to move forward.
It is hard to continue.
It is hard to decide what is meaningful. But, the growth and expansion only happens when you do.

And now, not only am I re-evaluating what is meaningful in my life again, I am walking my eldest daughter through the void as well.

She will never be the same.

I will never be the same because of what I witnessed in her life. This loss changed us all.

But, what does it all look like now? How does one create a "new way of being"? Because that is what is required. The old life is gone. The old dreams are gone because...

You are different.

The situation is different.

The meaning is different.

And because most of it is no longer RELEVANT.

You are creating your new way of being.

It all starts with determining what is NOW relevant and then deciding how to make each day meaningful again.

This is no easy task and not a path that is all that fun to be on.

It is about recreating your life.

For some, it will be refreshing because you didn't love the life that you were living before and for others, it will be really hard because you were loving the life you had.

I've experienced both.

When my baby died, we had been so excited. It was our first child together and our family would have been complete. Since we had just moved and I wasn't working yet, I was enjoying the time at home with my oldest that I hadn't had since she was little. We were all relishing in the anticipation of a new baby. And then, I left the hospital with a box, not a baby.

I had no idea what I wanted after it happened. None. My world seemed unrecognizable. I didn't have a baby. I didn't have a job to go back to. I didn't have a plan.

When I experienced my health crisis, the healing journey was one that I was relieved to be going on. I hadn't felt well for a long time and so having some answers and a treatment protocol that created progress within a few months gave me hope. I was still changed from that experience of the void and my life was radically different but it was easier to begin to find new meaning in my life. This was definitely a period of renewal.

I experienced that same feeling of renewed energy when I chose to get a divorce. It wasn't what I thought I would be doing but that decision of moving on from the marriage, freed me. While I didn't enter the void, I experienced a slight gap in the meaning of my life because it wasn't unfolding the way I had thought it would. But the experience in the gap was short-lived as rebuilding and creating a new way of life was such a relief and like a weight had been lifted.

And now, once again, with the death of my daughter's best friend, I didn't really feel like I "wanted" to be walking this path. I didn't want to be guiding her through this but I was. I didn't want to see how much pain she was in but I was. Life was definitely 'easier' for her and for all of us before this happened. Before this, I felt like I was clear on my purpose, I was clear on my message and I liked where our life was going as a family and what I was doing. It felt meaningful.

And then it didn't. There was that gap again.

And I know that the only way to continue to fulfill my purpose is to create meaning once again.

You do that by choosing to keep moving toward what you feel you want now.

The hardest part is that you are having to reframe, rebuild and recreate your life while you are in the the void and grieving heavily.

It is extremely difficult to see beyond what is happening right now and even consider what you might want.

When you are experiencing significant loss, how can one even consider thinking about the future when your world has fallen apart in the present.

When one goes through something life changing,

something that shifts everything that was important in your life, you must decide to consciously create meaning again.

To do that, you have to look to your future. But, if that feels too hard, start with what you know you don't want anymore in your life and move away from it.

You are not the same. You may or may not want the things that you wanted before.

My daughter is realizing that some of what she considered to be so important before holds little meaning now. She still has a desire to continue on with her university plans but a lot of what gave her life meaning, is no longer as relevant as it once was.

I experienced the exact same feeling each time I went through a loss, felt the gap in meaning in my life and entered into the void.

The way that I recreated my life each time was to face it and keep moving forward.

I accepted the loss.
I surrendered to the reality of it.
I released the need to know why.

You may decide that the emptiness or the void is where you want to be right now. That choice is up to you.

But, I will tell you that this loss in your life is an opportunity to understand how powerful you are. It is a way for you to shine brighter and share who you are.

You didn't have this experience so that you shutdown, you experience things so that you rise.

Will you choose to rise?

16

It
ALL
changes

A lot for me changed after the loss. It will for you too.

My relationships with people ended.

And new ones began.

My ability to put up with people's excuses and stories (including my own) became almost non-existent.

I went out less socially and created deeper relationships with those closest to me. My circle tightened even more.

My conversations got shorter and filled with less gossip.

And the ones I began to have created more impact and were more meaningful.

My work changed. What I once did as a marketing strategist, no longer meant anything to me. Everything I wanted had changed. I didn't know what I would do, but I knew that I couldn't go back.

My work is even more fulfilling now.

It all changed because the losses showed me more of who I was, who I wanted to be and what was truly most important to me.

I wanted to live more fully each moment.
I wanted to do more of what I was truly good at.
I wanted to create more impact.

You will experience this as well.

You may not know right away after your loss what you

truly want. This can take some time. The first step is to accept that everything has changed.

As you move through the void and the grief, the change in you will continue to be revealed. You will begin to uncover who you have become because of the loss you have experienced.

These changes in you and what you want create your new normal and because you can't go back, you might as well look forward.

The world is a place that is meant to be lived in.

17

It all FEELS foreign

When your life is in shambles and broken and those around you are happy and their lives appear to be wonderful, it is a weird space to reside in. It's awkward, strained and uncomfortable. It's hard to watch them live (even from a distance) and you can feel a bit jealous of how 'easy' their life is compared to yours.

Don't allow these feelings to drag you more into the depths of despair but allow them to give you hope that you will once again feel filled with meaning, vibrancy and passionate about life.

It is possible to achieve because you are seeing it happen all around you. (And some of those people have gone through exactly what you are experiencing and they are living their lives fully again.)

A few days after my daughter died, we went to a coffee shop. As I sat there and looked around, I felt even more lonely and even more empty (if that was possible). It was raining out. The people were busy talking about the weather and other useless bits of conversation (nothing of great value, just filling the air with words that wouldn't create much impact or so it seemed at the time).

I was suffering.
I was grieving.
I was trying to sort out what had just happened.
I was empty.
I was in the void.

And everyone around me, in that coffee shop, was living their everyday happy lives and it made me want to curl up in a ball and hide. They were laughing, talking loudly, eating donuts, drinking coffee and living.

I felt like I was dying inside.

I'm not sure I even lasted 15 minutes and told my husband that it was time to go.

There is a flood of emotions that happen as you begin to try to do more 'normal' things in the world.

I didn't feel comfortable out in the world. The world was still normal but I didn't fit anymore.

What was once important now wasn't and my world didn't feel the same. I noticed this with my work as well. I was a Marketing Strategist before my baby died and it just didn't hold the same meaning to me after her death. On that very day she died, I decided to never go back to my corporate career. And even when I was offered my dream job a year later, the one that I dreamt about in university and the one I had worked so hard to be offered, I turned it down. I wasn't going back. It wasn't me anymore. It was no longer my dream.

Sometimes, you don't get to make these radical life changes (like the one I did with my career) and so you must create new meaning within the activities you were doing before.

Will you look at them differently now? Yes.

Is that okay? Yes.

Can meaning be restored? Yes. Always.

The job, the relationships, and the daily tasks will all mean something different to you now. The eyes with which you view things has changed, the body with which you move through life has been altered and your heart has shifted.

All of this creates a significant change in your life and now, even some of your regular activities feel meaningless. This is normal and of course it would all feel different because you are changed.

The only way to create meaning again is to go through the daily motions, face each day and change the things that you feel called to shift.

This was one of the important things I knew I had to tell my daughter just after her loss. The "world" would be continuing on and it would feel like it was a foreign place to her. And even though her school friends and teachers were wonderful, so kind to her and supportive, their lives weren't impacted like hers was (her best friend lived in a different city than we did). Their normal lives would continue but her place in that 'normal" was not the same anymore. I knew that even with all of their compassion and support, it would be hard for her to find common ground with them for awhile and it was.

I think that this shift is not talked about enough. You experience a loss that creates a big gap in your life, you are in the void and you are grieving and to top it all off, the world becomes this place that no longer feels relevant.

You become the divorcee in the group of married or dating friends. It's lonely.

You are the one who has a restricted diet or activities because of your health issues. It's awkward to go out socially. Food and fun has created a divide now.

Someone close to you is newly pregnant but they don't tell you because they feel uncomfortable with the loss of your child and they don't want to make you feel worse.

The divide between your life and their lives continues.

The difference between what used to be and what is your new current reality deepens. When the scope of your world changes, everything you once thought was important shifts as well. This is one of the hardest parts to go through and understand because it can take weeks, months and years to rediscover and reclaim who you are in all of it.

You feel like a foreigner in your own life.

Nothing is familiar.
Nothing is the same.
Nothing is what you want it to be.

You are standing there wondering which way you should go now. There is no clear directions for how to go through something big like this. They tell you the steps and stages of grieving but that's not a road map to recreate your life, that's just the experience of grief.

You are now creating a whole new life and most of the time, it wasn't something that you wanted to be doing. You have to accept it (which is a big enough mental and emotional hurdle), then move past the resistance to the change that has occurred in your life and find the energy to begin to chart your course or at least move towards what feels lighter for you.

How do you actually do this when you feel so lost? You just begin.

I told my daughter in the first month of grieving to just keep going through the motions of getting up, getting ready and going to school. And with each new day and each time she did something "regular", she would begin to assimilate to her environment with who she was now. She would create her new normal by moving through it.

She didn't necessarily want to but even if she would have waited and hid her in room or if I would have hid in the house after my baby died, when I finally did step out into the world, it would not have been any easier.

I wouldn't have felt any better.

I don't believe I would have felt any less grief, felt any less awkward or any less uncomfortable had I delayed facing the world.

It would have held me in the void for longer.

You can't avoid the discomfort, you must face it.

That's the only way for the void to disappear.

18

What will you CHOOSE?

You are not the same after something like this. You never will be. This experience is now carved into your understanding and your life. That is not a bad thing, it is just what happens. It is the reality of your situation. What you do about it though is up to you.

The gap, the experience of the void and the significant loss that happened in your life, remains with you forever. It never goes away. How it feels will change but that's all. It is a part of you now.

I will never be the same mother after walking my daughter through her loss. I am not the same person I was before my debilitating health issue. I became a better version of me after my baby died when I decided to live more fully each day in honor of her.

When you create meaning in your life once again, you actually HONOR your experience of loss.

It is like showing appreciation for it.

These types of life experiences like deaths, divorces, job losses and health issues change you.

You get to decide how it will change you and if it will break you or make you.

In each circumstance, I decided that it would "make me" into a stronger, more powerful person.

That was a CHOICE. And not an easy one.

It would have been "easier" to crumble at the time, succumb to the pain and numb out.

Healing was actually harder than getting sick.

Facing each day and doing the stuff that creates a life felt like torture initially after my baby died.

When my daughter's best friend died, I could have chosen not to emotionally invest myself too much in making sure my daughter was okay and moving through her loss. The attitude of "she's young, she'll get over it and then hoping for the best" would have been way less work (in the present moment at least).

I quit my corporate career when my daughter died. I knew it wasn't what I was meant to BE in my life. I moved from an in-person training and consulting business to an online forum when I was on the road to recovery after being sick and was finally healthy enough to work again.

Now, even after this last life event, I am shifting my message and digging deeper into what I am called to do and the impact I am here to make.

I am even more dedicated to my cause, my purpose and the life that I want NOW from this new perspective.

I've been choosing to rise.

I am using the losses and the experience of the void to propel me to do and be more.

It would have been easier to hide in my room and not get out of bed the day after my baby died but I knew that I needed to lead my family and my oldest daughter through the loss and that meant getting up and taking the next step.

When I was really sick, it would have been easier to get sicker and sicker than follow the strict treatment protocol but I knew that I wasn't done yet in this life and that regaining my health was the only way to fulfill my purpose and be the mother I was dedicated to being.

And when my daughter's best friend died, I considered shutting down my business. I wondered about the poignancy and importance of the message I was telling and if it all really mattered.

But I didn't shut it down.

That would have been the easy choice.

I dug deeper instead.

I finished writing my story.

Rising UP is not the easier path but it is the one that you are meant to take.

It makes you stronger. It is the only way to live.

Will it feel really good all of the time? No, it won't.

Will you want to quit? Yes. And maybe even more often than you want to continue.

How do you keep going? You have to make a personal commitment to rise and to face your loss, your grief, and the gap in your life.

This is a process of digging deep and realizing that there is a bigger universal energy working for you and you can bow to it or you can use it.

CHOOSE to use it.

If this was meant to break you, you wouldn't be reading this right now.

While I don't have all of the answers and I can't speak to the grieving process from a medical standpoint, I do know that facing it and consciously choosing to move through it, healed my heart. If you feel that you need help, seek out a professional. You do not need to suffer alone and it is courageous and brave to ask for and seek out all forms of help.

What I do know from my experience is how to recreate meaning in my life. I've done it 4 times in the last 18 years. And each time, I found a deeper purpose, I knew more of who I am and I realized how strong and powerful I actually was.

This isn't the life that I thought I would have and I am sure that you feel the same way.

I certainly do not love what I went through and I never want to experience any of it again but during each experience, I was willing to face the pain and use it to understand myself more. From that, I created a life that I loved once again.

You can do this.
You can close the gap.
You can move through the VOID.

You can shift the trajectory of your life.
You can find meaning again.
You can show up for you on a daily basis.
You can rise.
You just have to CHOOSE.

You have to consciously decide whether your loss will make you or break you.

What is your choice?

I remember a conversation when my baby died with the nurse on duty that day who helped me prepare to deliver my stillborn baby. And I said...

> *"I will never move on from this experience (as I knew that it was forever a part of me now) but I will move forward and I do KNOW for sure that the reason why I am experiencing this will be revealed.*
>
> *And the strength that I gain from moving through this and growing from it and living more fully based on it will serve me and others in a big way."*

I knew this to be true even amidst all of the pain and the grief that I was experiencing.

I believed it.
I trusted in it.

You need to believe this too.

You need to know that this life event that you are

experiencing now or have just experienced will serve you at some point in your life.

That might be really hard to hear right now.
So, just take it in, remember it and know that one day you will go "that is what she meant".

Because it will happen. Your experience will help someone else as they go through theirs.

That I know for sure.

I heard this quote (I wish I knew who said it) and it is so true...

"When you are going through something, you are going TO something."

Like I said before, I thought my baby's death was for me understand how to live more fully and teach others how to do the same and now I know, more than 11 years later, that it was so I could walk my eldest daughter through the shocking loss of her best friend. I could not have helped her in the same way had I not gone through the loss of her baby sister.

I have used the lessons and the experiences that I learned from my divorce many times to help people find their way through theirs and also to remind me of who I want to be in my relationship. That loss has served me.

My health crisis revealed how important following the call of one's soul truly is; to live with purpose, to really appreciate what you have, and to honor your body for carrying you through each day. I am sure that there is much more to learn and understand as my healing journey continues.

The experience of my daughter's deep grief propelled me to finish writing this book. I am hoping that it will help you find your way and create meaning in your life once again after your loss.

19

You must TRUST

So how do you rise when you are in the void, when you feel stuck and when it all feels empty?

You must TRUST.

It will be hard to trust in a world that no longer feels familiar or friendly but you must try to trust it all.

Trust that there is a reason and that it will serve you.

Trust that the new meaning you create in your life will take you to bigger and better places.

Trust that this is what you signed up for and it will serve you and many others in some way.

Trust that you will find your way because you will if you want to.

Trust that it will get better because you choose it too.

Trust that you will know what to do.

Trust that meaning will return because you can create it.

Trust that you are powerful and can walk through this.

Trust that the universe will support you.

TRUST IN YOU.

You must choose to trust that your life can feel meaningful again.

20

Existing turns into LIVING

Initially after your loss, you just exist.

You go through the motions.
You face the day.
You do the "normal" stuff that doesn't really feel normal anymore but you do it anyways.

You smile.
You don't smile.
You fake smile.

Doesn't matter.

You just exist.

Until you begin to notice that there are minutes where you feel like you are living again not just existing.

You feel like yourself again.
You feel like you belong in the world and are apart of it.
You just aren't observing it anymore. You are living in it.

As these moments occur even more each day and over the course of many days, **existing turns more into living**.

And one day, you spontaneously smile and then you feel weird for smiling. You notice how good it feels to feel free from the grief and loss for just a little bit. And then the laughter comes back slowly at first and then even more and eventually it becomes easier to seek it again.

There is air again to breath (because in the void, there is very little air). There is brightness in the colors again (the void feels pretty grey). There is some possibility that you might be okay (hope begins to return) and that this new part of your life is doable.

You can have a life again and you are beginning to do it.

There's no timeline for this. It's your journey.

I know that the professionals give grief a timeline saying that the first year is the hardest. I believe that the grief lessens in its own time as you face your daily life more and more, as you continue to move through each day and as you increase your energy in your new normal.

The awareness that the first year is likely going to be the hardest is good. Use that timeline if it feels right to you but know that this is your journey and only you will know how long it will take for the grief to fade away. Only you know your experience, your loss and how it all unfolds in your way.

There is not a way, a box or a timeline for how grief happens for everyone and there is no "process" for recovering from a loss in your life. There is just the journey, your journey. And how YOU choose to face it and move through it.

Take as much time as you need. But, don't hide (it doesn't really help) and don't be too afraid to move forward.

No loss should take away your chance to live.

21

Continuing
FORWARD

You are not meant to be in the void for too long. You are not meant to stay there.

You have experienced the darkness and at some point you must follow the light. There is always a light (even if it is really dim) because there could be no darkness without light.

Follow that little voice, the intuition or the calling that you feel and take the next step. And then take the next one and the next one. And some days, you may take a few steps back or feel too tired and too alone to move forward and just accept that, knowing that tomorrow, you will rise again and take another step.

And as you move, you create meaning in your life again in small doses and then in bigger doses. Your steps will be bigger, the light will be brighter, and you will feel the pull of your new world and what it has ready for you.

You could spend a day, a few months or a few years in the void and you will only feel slightly different. The void is not where you heal or where your grief stops. You heal by facing each day, moving through it and creating meaning in your life.

This is your journey and your process.

The void isn't a place to reside. It isn't where the life you were meant for can be lived from.

The more time you spend there does not mean that you will feel better or that you will be healed when you leave from there.

When you have a wound and it heals there is almost

always a scar. The wound becomes part of you. Just like this experience, your loss, has become a part of you.

Healing from your loss doesn't mean you will ever be the same. Healing means that the wound is not gaping anymore and that the rawness of the emotion and the grief has lessened. But the loss (the scar), is something that will remain with you forever.

Choose to use your loss and how you have healed to serve, to love deeper and to live fuller.

So, start with a tiny step each day or take a leap (only you know what's right for you). But move. Begin creating the shift out of the void.

Only you can choose to move out of the void.

No one will save you. You have to find the strength to save yourself.

We all have this strength within us.

And know that as you move, meaning will slowly return, your energy and vitality will rise and with this new understanding of your life that is now is carved into the depths of your soul, you will continue to live.

And as you move, you will begin to live more fully and with purpose because you aren't here to exist without meaning.

22

Just MOVE

Rumi says:

"The wound is the place where the light enters you."

And he also says this:

"The cure for pain is in the pain."

I have learned more from my losses than from anything else in my life.

They have made me more compassionate, a better person, a more powerful soul and a stronger human being.

They have made me more resilient and far more capable to deal with my life on a daily basis.

When I was in the depths of my loss, I had no idea that I would ever be able to see the gift in these experiences and understand how they would continue to serve me in my life. I couldn't see how strong they would make me.

I am who I am today because of the wounds, the healing, the scars and the pain. I'm proud of who I've become through it all.

You will see the light.

You will diminish your grief with each painful step you take to face it and move forward. And you will eventually see the gift in it all.

Your only choice really when your life feels meaningless after a loss is to accept what is and surrender.

Then, you keep going on autopilot until it begins to feel

better, and you slowly move towards what feels okay and finally you find that meaning is being created because you are choosing to live your life.

Meaning resides in every choice you make.

Wanting for nothing and for it all to go back to the way it was is the natural response. The problem is that it can't go back to what it was before because you are no longer the same and your life has been forever changed with your loss.

Begin to ask yourself each morning "What's the one step I can take to create meaning again?" and then, do it.

Trust your gut.
Listen to your intuition.
Follow the whispers of your heart.
Allow yourself to be guided through this by the call of your soul and your deep knowing.

You get to decide how to move through this and the only thing that is important is that you begin to move again.

I know what you want.

You want to hold onto the vision of your life, the picture in your head of what once was or where you thought you were headed.

I wanted that too when my first marriage ended, when my baby died, when my health deteriorated and when my daughter's friend died. I wanted my old life back desperately. But, the truth is, you can't go back. Your whole vision for your life may be different now or even if you have the same vision that you had before the loss, how you will get there now is changed.

The dream you are holding onto of how it was 'supposed to be' actually stalls your healing journey because how it was 'supposed to be' is no longer your current reality and not possible anymore.

While going back is all that you desire, moving forward is all that is possible.

You may feel as though you are standing still but there is always a teeny bit of movement.

When you decide and choose to LIVE again, the steps become easier to take.

Sometimes it is hard to move forward and create meaning again because you feel guilty. Guilty to move through this and let go of some of the grief and the pain of the loss.

Sometimes, we think that if we move forward, we are "filling the gap in our lives" and that feels wrong. No one or nothing can replace that person or relationships that you have lost. There should be no guilt felt in living your life.

Creating meaning in your life again is NEVER about filling the gap. It is only about creating a new story and moving forward.

Your experience of loss is something that you now carry with you. You are not replacing anyone. You are not forgetting them. You are not dishonoring anyone. You are just starting to live again.

Do not feel guilty or ashamed of wanting your life back. You deserve it. And those you have lost would want that for you too.

23

Creating meaning AGAIN

At some point in the journey of your loss, you will realize that you are ready to begin really living again. It will be time to rise up and shine even brighter. You will accept that this is WHY this is happening for you.

You are the one who can change it all.

Meaning is created through taking action. Even if you don't know the "right" action to take.

Standing still and not being willing to take one step forward will keep you stuck in the meaningless void.

Meaning is created with movement.

Even if you can only move a little bit, it is in this movement, that meaning will begin to develop in your day.

How long will it take to feel "normal" again?

There is no answer for that. And there doesn't need to be one. Sometimes things just have to unfold and this is one of those things.

Why you are going through this is unanswerable and so is knowing what the length of time is that it will take for your life to feel meaningful once again and for you to feel 'normal' again.

But with every movement, meaning is right there with it. So the more you are willing to move through this experience and move forward (even if you can't see where that is to quite yet), the more meaning you will create.

Even if you decide that you hate where you have moved

to, you have created meaning because you know where you don't want to be.

Keep moving.

It will eventually get easier.

One day your life will feel normal again. It will be your new normal but it will be feel far more comfortable than it is right now.

24

Living YOUR Life

That day my daughter died, a part of me "died" too. Not in a bad way but in a way that shifted everything for me. In a way that has allowed me to create more meaningful impact.

It was in the deep, dark void, in that nothingness, I realized that I could create anything.

I declared on the day that she died that "I would move forward but I wouldn't move on". I knew that her life and her death would serve a very big purpose in my life.

I changed.
Everything changed.
Nothing looked the same.

Nothing mattered like it had before. And a lot of it mattered more.

I quit my corporate career that day.

I decided to stay home with my oldest daughter and put my attention on our family during the recovery from our loss.

I dug deeper into the meaning and impact of energy in our lives than I had before (Feng Shui was something that was fun and interesting before and after that day it became a WAY OF LIFE for me).

I remember looking into our front yard sometime in the first week after my baby died and saw some of the women who I had been in my Feng Shui class with tying red ribbons to my tree. I so wish I had a picture of that tree that I could share with you. They tied too many ribbons to count and I left them there until they all finally came undone and flew away.

Red is the color for power and strength in Feng Shui and it was their way of giving me power and strength to begin to walk through the loss. With every ribbon that would finally unknot itself and fly away, a little bit of me became free from the void.

I, to this day, don't know for sure who exactly tied those ribbons on that tree that night but if one of you or all of you are reading this, I express my deepest gratitude to you. Your act of kindness touched my heart and brings tears to my eyes to this day. The memory of that tree and those ribbons is entrenched in my heart forever.

Each and every day, so to this date that is over 4,000 days, I have thought of my baby and the impact she had on my life the day she died. That experience has guided my choices for my life and my commitment to live fully each day and fulfill my purpose.

Did I go off path at any point of my commitment to her to live fully?

For awhile, I would have answered yes. Upon reflection though, what I would have considered to be the "off path" part of my life actually taught me more about what my purpose was. I was on my path and experiencing my illness so that I could dig deeper into and understand more of the call of my soul.

Life and how you feel about it is truly about how you choose to look at it and how you choose to let it impact you. It is about you **allowing the awakening out the**

darkness of the experience and into the depths of the not totally known.

It is shining your light again fueled by your purpose and your will to live as much as you possibly can.

When you feel alone, remember, you are never alone.

You are always guided.

There is always someone there with you.

There is always someone who needs to hear what you have to say.

There is always someone to learn from.

There is always someone to teach.

There is always space for you to share who you are.

If I wouldn't have got a divorce, became sick, if my baby wouldn't have died, and if my oldest daughter wouldn't have lost her best friend, this book wouldn't exist in this form. I wouldn't be where I am at right now sharing this. None of this would have happened.

I can see that now but I couldn't see it when I was in the depth of my loss.

One day, you will see how this shifted the trajectory of your life and perhaps even answer the question of WHY it happened.

If it all didn't happen and I didn't experience the void and the loss of meaning in my life numerous times, I wouldn't be writing this and you wouldn't be reading it.

My life is more meaningful because of the losses that I went through.

Yours will be too.

It's funny how life later, with a different perspective, provides the answers and shows you that it all mattered and it needed to happen to get you to where you currently are.

Everything you have gone through has led you to now and to taking whatever your next action will be.

I really want you to find and discover meaning again in your life.

The whisperings of your intuition and the call of your soul are already telling you; the things that you love to do, the things that you are passionate about and the things that you are brilliant at are all clues to how you can shine your light.

And most importantly, be who YOU want to be.

This is your vigil.
This is your purpose.

Begin to live again.

Be more awake to what it is you truly want, how you want your life to be and the impact you want to leave on the world and be sure to LIVE FULLY.

Make your life your vigil. One that is filled with new

meaning because you have faced the void and you have been brave enough to move through it.

The only way through your loss, the grief and the void is to face it.

Kahlil Gibran, from the book The Prophet wrote:

"Your living is determined not so much by what life brings to you as by the attitude you bring to life; not so much by what happens to you as by the way your mind looks at what happens."

There is no right or wrong way to walk through this experience.

There is no right or wrong way to react, to grieve, and to experience loss.

There is no right or wrong way to recreate meaning in your life. It is just important that you do.

The truth is that it will never be "okay". You will never get over it totally. That's not possible. BUT...

You can rise. **You will rise.**

You can shine. **You will shine brighter.**

Pain is impossible to avoid. **Your suffering is optional.**

Your life is forever changed. And that's okay. It really is. **What you create next is up to you.**

What I want for you is to create something even more

meaningful. Use your experience of loss and of the void, to create a bigger ripple, to show people what living really means, to share your story and to be even more of who you were born to be.

You can. You will.

We stand together.
You are not alone.
You are never alone.

The void is dark but the light is filled with souls who have had an experience that has taken them to that same exact place. Seek them out. Surround yourself with people who understand and who have risen.

This will give you hope.

This will be provide you with a beacon of light.

This will give you strength to rise again.

Don't get stuck in the story of your loss and of the void.

This experience you have gone through is only one part of your life but it doesn't have to be the rest of the story.

Don't let this be your whole story.
Don't let it define you.
Let it move you.

You've got this.

I know you do.

Even on the days when you think you don't, you do.

Let the meaning unfold again.

Allow yourself to live.

Shine your light.

You can do this.

You can create your life anew. One that is overflowing with meaning and purpose again.

I know you.
I was you.
I rose.
You can too.

Give yourself permission.

Permission to live again.
Permission to love again.
Permission to laugh again.
Permission to smile freely.
Permission to enjoy each day.

And most importantly, permission to move through this and recreate your life.

Start choosing this next part of your journey. CHOOSE to keep living YOUR most meaning-filled life.

With love,

Jill

One final thing...

Because I know what you are going through, I wanted to give you something very special. I enlisted a talented composer to create 3 very meaningful meditations to accompany this book.

I want to gift them to you.

My hope is that they provide you with some peace and the inspiration needed to move through your loss and to create meaning in your life again.

You can download them for free at
www.jillethier.com/gift

I would be honored to hear how this book has impacted you. Email me your story at jill@jillethier.com and share with me how you will rise. And be sure to share this book with anyone you know experiencing a loss in their life.

I would love to connect with you on social media. You can find me at Jill Ethier on Facebook and Instagram and listen in to my podcast Ninja Jill KNOWS on iTunes or Stitcher for daily inspiration to live more fully.

*You will find a way through this and
you will be stronger for it.*

Sending the brightest of light your way.

~ JE

ABOUT THE AUTHOR

Jill has created her life with her 3 girls and her husband on an acreage close to where she grew up. She spends her days focusing on her work, spreading her message and watching the girls run, play and live their best lives.

She shares her love of blending energetic and strategic tools and techniques to create the life you desire with her clients in her online programs, on her podcast Ninja Jill KNOWS, in her speaking engagements and within her one-on-one and group consultations and virtual workshops.

She writes, speaks and shares her message daily about listening to the call of your soul, fulfilling your purpose, being who you were born to be and creating the life that you truly want.

To learn more about her, the programs she offers and to sign up for her weekly emails, visit www.jillethier.com.

.

Made in the USA
Columbia, SC
03 February 2018